Something about Living

AKRON SERIES IN POETRY

Something about Living

Lena Khalaf Tuffaha

 The University of Akron Press
Akron, Ohio

ISBN: 978-1-62922-273-8 (paper)
ISBN: 978-1-62922-274-5 (ePDF)
ISBN: 978-1-62922-275-2 (ePub)

A catalog record for this title is available from the Library of Congress.

∞ The paper used in this publication meets the minimum requirements of ANSI/NISO z39.48–1992 (Permanence of Paper).

Cover image: *Los Troncones*, 30" x 36" acrylic on canvas by Soraya Farha. Cover design by Amy Freels.

"Moving Towards Home" from *Directed by Desire: The Complete Poems of June Jordan*, Copper Canyon Press © Christopher D. Meyer, 2007. Reprinted by permission of the Frances Goldin Literary Agency.

Epigraph on page 3 from *After the Last Sky*, by Edward Said. Copyright © 1999 Edward Said. Reprinted with permission of Columbia University Press.

Something about Living was designed and typeset in Garamond by Amy Freels, printed on sixty-pound natural, and bound by Baker & Taylor Publisher Services of Ashland, Ohio.

Produced in conjunction with the University of Akron Affordable Learning Initiative. More information is available at www.uakron.edu/affordablelearning/

For Raya, Reema, and Renda

because I need to speak about home
I need to speak about living room
where the land is not bullied and beaten into
a tombstone
      —June Jordan

Contents

III.

Transit

A hoopoe leaves
a feather on the cusp
of a hillside, a temple
I've chosen of unremarkable rock,
its particular cradle of light.

Mine is a story of never
being able to stay long enough
to be known, of noticing
all the smallest relics.

In the rock's shadow a cluster of wild cyclamen,
or what could be
geraniums, what might be foraged
for sustenance, what might be
pressed for keeping.

I.

Each Palestinian structure presents itself as a potential ruin
—Edward Said

Variations on a Last Chance

The fence does not hold.

The wire sheds its barbs, softens to silk thread.

The snipers run out of bullets.

The desert, as it always has, of its volition, blooms.

The snipers are distracted, sexting their girlfriends.

The snipers' eyes are blinded by smoke from our burning tires.

The snipers wonder if they will ever see the end of us.

The fence does not hold.

The snipers take a lunch break.

The bullets melt in their chambers.

The bullets disintegrate when they reach the word PRESS on Yasser's vest.

The news finally breaks the stillness around us.

The bullets will themselves away from the boy's skull.

The boy's sandals sprout wings and he hovers above the bullets' path.

The snipers lose interest in shooting at medics evacuating the wounded.

The snipers make eye contact with one of us and see.

There are enough saline bags at the hospital.

The snipers shoot and miss and miss and miss.

We outrun the snipers.

We bury the dead at the fence, let their roots reach the other side of home.

Portraits of Light

Then

The light is a molten weight, a mountain
of thirst. Of the old stones of their houses,
it makes an ocean, azure dissolving into distance.

And they are a chiaroscuro huddled on the arthritic bridge,
bodies scant as bedclothes, damp and wrinkled
in the throes of nightmare, bodies trudging
in low relief against limestone.

Who spoke first as they walked? Did the boy
in slippers shuffle ahead asking
after his bicycle? Did the old man mutter
end-of-days verses between sobs? The sun scores
tender scalps, inscribes legends on a map of loss.

Now

The light is damask draped on the clothesline.
Tea glasses touch with castanet swiftness, a mint haze
floats over the women's words. The gate groans
open and the music of slender heels on tiles ushers in the evening.

Tea darkens in the pot as cicadas prepare
their supplications, mosquitos ready for their night raids.
One of the women slides the deck out of its box, halves it,
begins to deal. Another reaches for her monogrammed lighter,
their laughter a rustle of curtains drawn.

String-of-pearl smiles enrobed in scarlet give way
to cigarette kisses. Smoke undulates, threads
between soft curls and crepe collars.
Manicured fingers wave fans of kings and queens.

Later

The light is irrelevant, though it fills quiet rooms of departure,
great cones of it, dust mites wild with gold.
How was the news delivered? Inscribed
in the ink of dreams or settling in the dregs of coffee cups?
Sick with yesterday's fever,
a newspaper yellows in the stairwell.

Bespectacled experts survey the patterns in prayer beads
for signs of structural damage, of impending collapse.
There is no wind to carry omens through the window.
It hasn't rained in years and the locusts
walk among us, sunlight ricocheting off their medals.

Beit Anya

The name of my father's village
speaks of the misery of pilgrims unwelcome
for their poverty, a thorn

-strewn hillside to keep them
at a distance from the house
of god for fear of their disfigurement.

All language is littered with corpses
of words, the shrouds we make
for them, the sacred oils we spill

to anoint, to embalm. Beit a home;
ancient breath and second
letter of ancestry. Home of unripe figs

or of suffering? Or of the tribe
who amassed enough gold
and armor to consolidate a story?

I need no dictionary
to parse the twin spirits of Anya—
that affliction and caregiving

are one vector, measured in cubits
or years of prayer
occluded from the sanctuary. In my father's childhood

soldiers clamored the rocks
to Lazarus' tomb. He longed for
lamb and spiced rice instead of the bones

the wealthy uncles sent after feasts
for a broth to stay ten mouths. He dreamt
and wandered the olive groves.

He went to school in the city
of seventy names. All language is volition,
the rising up of a body

thought lifeless, the summoning
of a spirit from sepulchral silence. A village
might be known for derelict light, for footsteps

of supplicants, its dead a transom
fastening it to memory. Before his own father died,
the family kept a dog to herd cattle

and hold coyotes at the edges of the fields.
Prince—my father told us the animal's name,
a frail laugh uttered as a third transfusion raised him,

again from the precipice. A proper English name,
a protest, *even our dog, awlad al kalb,*
and when the canine sank his teeth

into the soldier's shin, my grandfather
protected his own, told the soldier who had come for blood
that to shoot his dog he'd have to kill its owner first.

All language is legend—we grow into its landscapes.
House of Misery for want, for death's
early visits and a dearth of miracles. My father says

the soldier returned, smirking,
with a thick slab of meat that Prince could not resist.
Our derivation of meaning—the study we make

of moments—travels the empires engraved
in our palms. That a poison robbed a boy
of his dog is both calamity and marginalia.

All language is oracular—
we are forever
burnishing the wound, readying the chasm.

Dialogic

However broken the sentences
you believe them preferable to silence

the kind that crowned
the remains of the village

Kabri was without a fight

or the park now at its entrance,
past the foundation stones and beneath the picnic benches,

to the fig trees huddled over headstones.
Kabri looms large over heavy branches,

the name a contraband clutched in throats.
Homeland of water, the guide said that

Reshef, who was together with his brother, got hold
of a few youngsters, lined them up

the springs of Kabri quenched all the villages
of Akka, moistened the lips of morning.

He recounted their names
عين مفشوح عين فنارة عين العسل

fired at them with a machine gun. He was a brave fighter.

Songs of plenty their syllables cascading
over us in light soft as apricot skins.

I wonder at these park benches
perched above the ruins of another woman's home.

Our friend urged us to proceed, it was not too long
before they took us and a few others.

You unsheathe your fear when the body count rises.
You calibrate majorities, try to mitigate the distance

from doorstep to checkpoint. I hear
the language of sunbirds trilling in the carob trees,

There a Jewish officer put a gun to my husband's neck,
"You are from Kabri?"

someone had to choose
to position a park bench with a view of the village

took away my husband, Ibrahim, Hussain, Khalil al-Tamlawi, Uthman, and Raja.

cemetery, of the monument to the conquering
brigade. Your fears demand fortification, and I'm left to exhume

An officer asked me not to cry. We slept in the orchards
that night. Next morning

the names beneath your settlements, to dust
time off their letters. Find me

> *on the way to the village courtyard I saw Um Taha.*
> *She cried and said,*

a language for us to grieve those whose children
wait precious few kilometers from the park benches, relegated

> *"You had better go see your dead husband." I found him.*
> *He was shot in the back of the head.*

to a camp's sewage-filled alleys, to half-streets,
shuttered beneath a net of refuse, the thorn-strewn path. Enough

for each of us, let this language be enough
or let silence
                final, diluvial.

When The Sky Is No Longer

a womb, prayers now besieged

inside your throat hum over whistles

and shrieks—the long howl

puncturing what was.

Silence is the first casualty.

You no longer fear the clamor,

not because you are brave, but

because you've learned that death arrives

noiselessly, hovering

in the bowels of a missile,

that the clamor means

you are alive and someone else is dying.

You note the bleakness of your own heart

wanting to live in spite of this.

Maritime Nocturne

Across the sea floor
limbs curl through ink clouds,

settle near an old trunk
letting go its treasures.

Sodden maps surrender
their borders, and silver frames

tarnish. Currents swallow
dark clots, and across Gaza the rain

sorties over new monuments
of ash, open wounds of rubble.

Waves buckle under
the weight of swollen vessels,

flayed carcasses hauling
hundreds of lives

to shorelines where no one
looks forward to their arrival,

relentless survivors, white-knuckle
grasping at stars, reaching

for the buckle of Orion's
belt, the cleft of his boot.

Even on nights when
there is no anchor, the brine

of a dream consumed
by the sea, salt like shards

on parched lips is gentler
than the sulfur of prayer—

the dry scorch of waiting for mercy.

A Single Word: *Home*

Darwish Cento

Denuded of my name, of belonging,
childhood memories grow up in me,
one day following another.

In the deep horizon of my word
I have a moon
and it is as tiny as a sesame seed.

I have learned all the words needed
for a trial by blood. If I return one day,
take me for a kindling in your fire.

I am aged, a fog veils me,
facing the dusk and the cannon of time,
the fields of wheat, the white graves.

Free, I stand beside my freedom.
I am known to all the songs of rain,
all the prisons, all the borders.

I must be worthy of my mother's tears.
For my name, I shall choose letters of azure,
the birds that chased after my palms.

What will we do before this death?
We are dust's bygone neighbors.
You who stand in the doorways, come in!

Fragments from a Sudden Crescendo

At the Gate of Mercy

they are firing tear gas,

they have pushed us back

to re-envision

landscape with an architecture

of return. We gather

our stones, have

been told to wait,

they have pushed us

back with tear gas   stun grenades.

Stadium seating, torpor

of eyes trained on us, dispatches

filed in guileless

verbs. Of Mercy, singed

and defiant, we remain,

preparing our breakfast

as they fire tear gas   stun grenades   live ammunition.

Gates crenelated, sky widening,

sultans stir in their sleep,

offer archways to lift nightmares

from their brows. Museumed graves

intone a call to prayer

for the living. We perform our ablutions

in tear gas

our limbs stun

our hearts grenade

our wounds live

freedom ammunition.

Threads

Some people can go up to twenty seconds

      without breathing especially in the middle

            of the night.   I was writing a poem then

an arrhythmia set in. It's about refugees, but it's also full

      of paranormal phenomena. It's about food scarcity, and

            the thing is, it can't save us. I believe

in the spirit world. I have no desire

      to encounter its edges, to graze the lips of the cauldron,

            flames braiding and unbraiding in my throat. Let us plan

to decolonize our spaces. Let us avoid those who personify,

      imposters rearranging words in a style that vanishes after

            it's spoken, without a pulse at its heart. Are we in love, any of us,

inside the rooms we inhabit? Is love the first

      casualty of our times? Let us plan, brothers and sisters,

            a museum heist or a freedom march, a lapis lazuli

set in metal that will not tarnish, scored

      thrice in the way our grandmothers tattooed their chins.

            You cannot swallow a life

this large, the bones no longer
        tender, the body reordered
                by what it carried.

On the Thirtieth Friday We Consider Plurals

At the border, a flock of journalists.
A sacrifice of tires burned behind us.
Beneath the picnic tents, a funeral of families.
What else will we become in Gaza if we gather,
if we carry our voices to the razored edge?
We were met by a gallop of prayers,
clamoring recitatives puncturing the shroud
of humid air. We were met by a delirium

of greetings, peace-be-upon-us surreal
between embraces, the horizon locked
and loaded. What is upon us
will require mercy. Let the plural be
a return of us. A carnage of blessings—
bodies freed from broken promises,
from the incumbrances of waiting.

First Generation

Our parents told us: if we left, it was for fear

of what might fall,

the structures that house us,

the sky itself, breeched, defenseless.

And if we remained, it was for fear

of what would be taken, the orchards

that raised us, the catalog

of wildflowers we foraged

after the last rains, the names

inscribed on grandparents' headstones.

So little is spoken of

love and its fractured geography.

Like all good refugees, our parents teach us

remembering

how it is forgetting's successful twin, how it graduates

from the best university, makes a life for itself

in tech and finance, in arts and letters, and when our fingers

part to examine it, what we've gripped like the edge

of a lifeboat, like a lantern, our hands are empty,

a canvas the color of the stones of our villages.

II.

و نريد أن نحيا قليلا, لا لشيئ
بل لنرحل من جديد
—محمود درويش

Enter Here

Our city gates are named for animals
carved into its stones, for spiritual
states, for exile's destinations. Everyone
loves a survivor. They scan for bruises—
signs of process, hymns of futurity.
Not all cities are built to shelter gods.
Ours hosts neighborhoods of divinities.
Our city grows legends in its alleys,
blinds conquerors with its light. Survivors make
endurance imaginable. Beyond
the eastern gates there is a prison named
for a pilgrim's ancestry, a prison
famous for innovations in torture.
Here, innovation culture reigns supreme.

To Be Self-Evident

After Edward Said

Every empire tells its subjects a story
of revelation. The trees let down
their aging leaves, listless
in late drought. The children thrive on filtration,
their classroom air and their selfies sanitized.

Every empire seems invincible
as its borders submerge, its manicured hillsides
incinerate between guaranteed
next-day deliveries.

Every empire eulogizes
its value system, splurges
for pyrotechnics, decorates
its mausoleums for the holidays.

Every empire turns
against its colonies, cradling
the embassy's crystal in bubble wrap,
packing extra treats for the dogs on the evacuation flight home.

Every empire promises
a revolution against itself. The children
are tasked with designing the future, growing
walls of hydroponic greens,

rebranding old protest anthems.
Every empire denies the iceberg
it crashes into, hires a chorus, funds the arts.

Every empire sings itself a lullaby.

This Day Our Daily Bread

on the most recent largest mass shooting

Today you saved on investing, and the side effects
may include fever dizziness shortness of breath
you should lie down
and find out what your sleep number is
you should shelter in place
while every vote counts.

Today is paid for by the people.
Relief is slow when you are an island
and the death toll, like the hurricane count,
is rising, but most of these claims
have not been verified.

Today is an offering that can be
redeemed at participating locations
while supplies last, though reports indicate
the gunman worked tirelessly.

Today was confirmed by multiple sources
and thoughts and prayers have been filed.

Today is an exclusive report we learned about
while getting the tough stains
out. Ranking members had no comment
but the pastor at the crime scene said:
"I do not understand, but I know my god does."

In Case of Emergency

M.K., 1938–2023

This is how you open the box
when I am no longer here.

One of these might be the combination:

1975
The year you were born

1967
The year we lost the rest of our country

1936
The year your grandmother swallowed her gold coins
to hide them from the soldiers

This is how you keep yourself
safe, keep parts

of yourself in different boxes.
Trust no one
with everything

1949
The year my father died

1979
The year the checkpoint taught you
The difference between your name and your passport

1999
The year the last of our olives were uprooted
and the wall obscured Jerusalem

This is how you know it will end:

When night falls the windows of the city
become mirrors, a key recalls
the shape of its doorway, the stones of this land
nestle in young hands.

Envelope

It happens that survival is no more than ink
                        and weight of rubber stamps arranging freedoms
into a precision of entrances and exits It happens
                        that a woman named for the camp where she waits
embroiders more than dresses more
                        than the flora of a land that has not seen
eglantines for years of rubble that has unhoused the rock
                        sparrow and starved it that an epistolary
love becomes artifact its promises fading
                        its days a siege of unanswered questions
its pages a street where we decide finally to stay
                        it happens that a beloved might be granted passage
just before the building folds on itself
                        in three sections or just before words dissolve
and shrapnel rain disperses the living It happens
                        that what was taken from us in waiting cannot
be given language that to seal an envelope
                        the tongue though traditionally the site of first touch
may be insufficient a drought or network
                        of acid canyons score its surface and knotted beyond
prayers for loosening it becomes too heavy
                        and which one of us makes it to the border and which
one of us will become the story and
                        and where will they send us

It happens that an envelope can wait

                    in an abandoned drawer it can be too late to write

what we have lived it happens that a hunger can live on in

                    a room unpeopled an open mouth a soundless gasp

In Palestine There

after Myung Mi Kim

is no post
is no post-traumatic stress disorder
is only now and letters
if they arrive
might be decades old

                          at age 70 this is the first time for her to see
what would the sea be if we were near it
change   chart   what sound do we
transcribe   transient   transforming
formative   inform
speak and it is
instead   steadying   scrutiny   routine
                          the route is closed by military vehicles
refuse   refuge   fugue   rife with
               she is three wars old and can tell by sound which missile
fire
                          his face made unrecognizable
effacement
                          what is meant by from the river
overt   other   gather   gate
ground   work   waiting
               she has survived hours beneath the rubble but now doesn't speak
noise   news   knows   oh say
can you see
once we leave a place is it there?
At the edge, even the sea

On Translation

Even when he told her
it was imminent, Mira refused
to break up with him. Readers might be
moved if they imagine the fiancé
had a fatal injury or a terminal illness.
Mira tells the reporter that her fiancé entrusted
a counselor at the courthouse where he tried to break off their engagement
with his last will and testament.

Tell her she's the best girl in the world.
Tell her she is the most beautiful.
Tell her. Tell her these are my exact words.

The word *martyrdom* fails
Mira's heart and her beloved's.
The word *trauma* does, too.
Mira says sometimes he would talk about settling down,
about a home, but he also kept trying to let her go.
You have a life to live, you're too young to be a widow.

His last words to Mira
are where language breaks. أما أنا طريقي معروف شو هو
To translate is to believe there is a reader.

When he turned to leave the courthouse,
the counselor ran after him with the final
question in her arsenal, but the drones
circling overhead drowned out his reply.
Don't you want to wait,
to see her before you go?

The narrow alleys of old Nablus
are crosshatched in light and jasmine vines.
That a heart will not back down
when an armored vehicle barrels towards it
is also a love story.

Mira said, *I'll be a martyr's wife, then.*
In the final hour, her father called the fiancé
and translated: *Listen, son. Whatever happens*
to you happens to us.

In 1998, as Israeli settlement building in the occupied West Bank and Gaza accelerated, American luxury brand magazines featured an advertisement for tourism in Israel with the slogan "No one belongs here more than you do."

Triptych

Under Appropriate Auspices

No one belongs here more than you do shall be subjected to torture
or to cruel, inhuman, or degrading treatment or punishment.

Every no one belongs here more than you do has the right to leave any country,
including his own, and to return to his country.

No distinction shall be made on the basis of the political, jurisdictional, or
international
status of the country or territory to which a person no one belongs here more
than you do

Nothing in this Declaration may be interpreted as implying for any State, or
person, any right to engage in any activity or to perform any act aimed at the
destruction of any of the rights no one belongs herein more than you do

Resolves that, pending agreement on no one belongs here more than you do
detailed arrangements among the Governments and authorities concerned,
the freest
possible access to Jerusalem by road, rail, or air should be accorded to all
inhabitants of
Palestine;

We have no agenda other no one belongs here more than you do to meet our
statutory duties

Resolves that the refugees wishing to return to their homes and live at peace with their

neighbors should be permitted to no one belongs here more than you do so at the

earliest practicable date,

Erosion

No one belongs here more than you do

No one belongs here more than you do

No one belongs here more than you do

No one belongs here more than you

No one belongs here more than you

No one belongs here more than you

No one belongs here more than

No one belongs here more

No one belongs here

No one belongs here

No one belongs

No one belongs

No one be

No one

No
....

Reclamation Cento

In the mirror of my heart you can find no shelter.

One woman loses 15 maybe 20 members of her family, one garden at a time.

I belong to the road and nothing belongs to me.

Out here, eyes find the edge that isn't one.

I want nothing more from the passing days than the aroma of coffee,

stronger than memory, and sadder than sadness.

We are all waiting for you, you who have come so far.

Do not underestimate this rubble.

Maqluba

The congressman began his remarks to a room of refugees and their children who had invited him to share their national dish after the most recent massacre with *ultimately* then ran his tongue across his front teeth *there is a special relationship* then a slight twitch of his chin and increased activity all around his mouth. *Look* and his left hand flew up like a shield as he jammed his pinkie fingernail beneath his top lip and excavated the gum line. *I get it* from behind his hand. Several of the elders leaned forward in their chairs to decipher his muffled pronouncements. *Here's what I will say* emphasis on *will* so that the room was now focused on what he wouldn't say then finally a moment of audible relief as the shard of almond was dislodged, restoring peace to canine and incisor. Gracious in victory, he placed it ever so gently in his palm. His words dropped off as he examined it, and for a moment it was just the congressman and the almond in the room. When an elder cleared his throat and snapped him out of his reverie, he looked up at his hosts seated around the table and at the collapsing dome of fragrant rice, eggplant, and chicken at its center, and he remembered to offer the traditional greeting *you and I can agree the best hope is a return to negotiations.*

Dendrology

We are five in the van, three of us southerners or maybe two; one has migrated west.
Americans now, our shoes and our proclivities indicate, practitioners
of liminal freedoms. We can identify and describe what will undo us.
We upend our stories with bilingual euphemisms. One recalls the curses
of a father. Another re-enacts his child's slippage between words, mother-
tongue, and moment. *What kind of tree are these*, I ask, noting the lacy canopies
that shade the sidewalks. It is engineered to look accessible, the American
city, the distance from one to another in this country. We know our names
are gray zone enough to invite exercises of classification. They may
or may not be oak, though one of us doubts, lists the qualities of bark, of leaves.
Likely pecans, a southerner suggests, recalls a childhood neighbor's front yard tree.
Years ago my mother confided, as we drove north past a pleat of snow-capped cedars:
Some mornings I imagine it all returned, asphalt pulled up with our structures and
transgressions undone. We are always learning the original names of trees.

Notes from the Civil Discourse Committee

A Thorn Crown of Sonnets

It was "the first time"—I took my daughter
to a protest. She was three weeks old and
my ligaments, my language still loose,
the ground beneath me precarious—
"I was in a state of knowing"—what it
means for life to claim you as a vessel,
for my body to become a border,
the truth of—"the world she had crossed into"
"can we begin" —with the children picked off
across the barbed wire fence by snipers
"I recognize this is difficult"
—to question the smallest of givens
"none of the words" you speak ever name us.
Do you understand why some things must break?

*****

"Do you understand" why some things must break?
—I have tried "to be an American"
—It was a posture built on compliance
and selective memory that skin and
origin story do not preclude me
from "eligibility for a dream"
—that a parent's exile can be upcycled
"a life in another landscape"—It was

a posture of last resort "The first time
I met an elected official"—was
at a protest "he was seated on a stage"
—for a ceremony I was outside
—reporters asked *why are you here today?*
"because they are dancing on our graves"

*****

Because they are dancing on our graves
when they aren't bulldozing them, elections leave
bitter dregs in the mouth. A few years later
we arrive at *no he's a decent man*—
as opposed to an Arab "one candidate
said of another"—defending him
to his own kind—I have been corrected
whenever I recount this American
experience. "Even the decent"-as-
opposed-to-an-Arab man goes on
in the vernacular of his people
to bomb bomb bomb. And still "the longing for
his era of such decorous"—death thrives.
—it was a posture of late empire.

*****

It was a posture of late empire
to "resist settler colonialism"
—while making friends and influencing
people. "Why am I here today? I'm asked
this question often"—by those who made it
inevitable. "And yes, I would love
to *go back home*"—even that dismissal
requires something other than "peace."—More
like a new language for the past that blooms
wild on our hillsides—crushes verb tenses—
an unsettling—a fresh old map—or just
your exquisite absence where it has been
needed. The departure of your shadow
starving us for light, wilting all that lives.

Iconic

for Ahed Tamimi

Tonight/between translations/when we carried a poem/from one country/
into another language/where perhaps the imperative doesn't land/with the
same iron blow/as the original/I recounted the story of a theater of people
listening to a young poet become/apocryphal/and gathering his lines/as fast
as they could and then I tried/to say that the one/word he used for writing
and recording/would require a sentence or a story or a pantheon/to capture
it and I thought of the word/I have come to hate most in English/which is
peace/because it is always pointed at my skull/and I am supposed to want/it
more than my own name.

//

Tonight a blood moon pulsed above the prison cells/where nimble fingers
threaded beads the colors/of a flag/and steadied themselves for the moment/
after the door slams again and they stay/behind it/measuring shadows and
memorizing/the laws that are broken to keep them there.

//

Tonight a girl with a mane of wheat-colored hair slept in her own bed in the
silence between invasions.

//

To night and the poem/of a man who loved a woman across the barbs
delineating/history/poem that became a song/poem placed squarely
between a rifle/and his beloved's eyes/the color of honey/poet/who in an
aging photograph seemed more/a boy in outsized glasses and shoes/walking
towards the lines he would write/the way any of us/otherwise rational beings
might/walk into the waves knowing/we have never been able to swim/our
waists lassoed by threads of moonlight/the bell of our questions/surging
inside the cave of the body/the table of what is possible/shifting, spilling over.

//

To night and/the ravages of its insatiable/mouth and lightlessness where
poets/and children who will not give up the words that speak them/are
swallowed. It is possible/outside this cathedral/of stars and glimmering/
planets, it is possible to imagine that fear/inflicted on the body/by sound
grenades and strip searches/by shackles and threats of oh/the rosiness/of
your skin do you/burn easily in the sun/it is possible to imagine that these
could break/us too

//

Night and the day that follows are both promise/and prison. I tried/to say
this about translating/the poem/about breaching the waves/about painting
a girl's/face onto a wall to frighten/a monster/about lingering at the empty
chair/where the departed poet's jacket is perfectly folded beneath/the
spotlight/I understand/this desire/ that cannot have/enough for want of
light and access/to the sea/I understand it carves icons/out of our bones/
ululates as the fallen are returned/to their mothers/dances/the same dance at
weddings and funerals/I understand/but it might not translate.

Sfumato

To speak with ease as if
English were your own.
To realize that what is praised
in the spaces

where belonging is most desired
is always precision, moving
left to right across a page,
a clarity that startles, succinct

translations coalescing at their most needed.
To understand that the shortest distance
between disappearing and desire
is a turn of phrase.

To achieve language
acquisition untarnished by family or history.
To own the loss that such ease broadcasts.
To return nearest the source in order

to root ancestral seasons in the hearts
of your children only to be offered
a job teaching English to their peers
because you speak it fluently, which is to say

without accent,

which is to say in the manner

of our most recent masters,

which is to say your articulation

is unhindered by residual evidence

of your heritage, which is

another way to say

you didn't get to grow up here.

Long Distance

Oh the good times spent with you—
God bless them with a gentle rain.
—Ibn Zaidoun

In this country language only leaves me
tongue-tied. My words a bright nasturtium
in the clutches of a thousand spider mites. This poem is not
a passport, though, I confess, I miss the days
of anthems, the schoolyard's morning lines.
Hours slow-drip into one another, their margins
softer, their caverns deepen. Why do I long for
the crumbling staircases that many are fleeing, how to grow
out of this tawdry ache? In memory summers
are trimmed with geraniums and blue jasmine spilling
over a garden wall. To remember
is a discipline of waiting and distance. Everything
unravels, even those who grow up
where they belong must flee,
the songs echo in the valley but we can
no longer risk breathing. Now fevers
indicate a danger it's too late to deter.
This summer is cold. What to grow in intermittent
sunlight? Who imagines this poem is for them?
Whatever histories we were raised on have come
to an end, whoever raised us lives on in our eyes.

Other Words for Blue

There is a doe in the wildwood
      The doe has mirror-glass eyes
            When I met you I dreamt of trampling the garden I planted

Doe is another word for female
      Doe is a homonym for the origin of bread
            When I met you the scent of your skin filled my lungs

Doe eyes are an old-world measure of beauty
      The women line their eyes with blue antimony
            When you say, "I love you," your eyes are closed

Naturalists ascribe superior night vision to the doe
      Arabic names seven distinct phases of night
            When I met you a civil twilight was fading to blue

I know the story of a woman named after the land she inhabited
      I line my eyes and the history of sand glints back at me
            When I met you I danced at the edge of a room

Omens are an old-world method of forecasting
      In the old city, a blue-eyed woman reads the dregs of my coffee
            When you say, "I love you," I taste cardamom

I know the story of a woman named for the antimony in her eyes
      Arabic names a bird for the blue feathers in its wing
            When I met you a moonbridge cleaved the water

Kohl is finer than bread flour
      Antimony is extracted from the stones of Ithmid
            When I met you sand lingered in the hem of my dress

The blue-eyed woman sees two paths in my coffee dregs
      The women in the room cup their fortunes in their hands
            When you say, "I love you," a hemstitch breaks on my lips

A doe makes a home by bedding in dense foliage
      I know the story of spears disguised in the palm fronds
            When I met you my words were an ink stain

Ancestors lined children's eyes with antimony for protection
      Arabic names a beloved after our eyes
            When I met you it was the season of the blue-veined nigella

Doe is another word for mother
      There is a chance our children will have motherless tongues
            When you say, "I love you," you drop the I

Language is another word for flight
      Birds are an old-world talisman
            When I met you I breathed the last of the incense

The blue-eyed woman tells me a man stands at the end of one path
      I know the story of a woman who paid for the answers with her eyes
            When I met you I traced the lines in my palms

There is widespread ignorance about the levels of lead in kohl
      Arabs say fate is a creature nestled at our throats
            When you say, "I love you," I dream a field of stones

The blue-eyed woman tells me a candle flickers at the end of the other path
      The women line the bread with nigella seeds for blessings
            When I met you Altair crowned the sky

A doe will graze on a moonlit night
      Come the stars now, softening the silhouettes of trees
            Your love is an old song at the blue doors of night

The woman with antimony visions becomes a namesake
    The nigella, blooming, is named love-in-a-mist
        Our constellation is a restless blue-winged bird

When I met you I burned my translations
    In the old city, the blue-eyed woman signaled:
        the other path, the man standing at the center of the flame.

Madwoman Ghazal

It is true we named our own sea dead
but in the houses nearby the bougainvillea flourishes.

On the shore we call this marvel majnouneh.
The sea is a body keening, glistening in sunlit flourishes.

The tree loosening long branches over the wall is always a woman.
In the sea's azure declination, a mineral kingdom flourishes.

Sulfur sorrow, fishless stillness is our sea.
Around the tree, the desert unfolds in sweltering flourishes.

In midday our sea is a silver tray, salt-crusted.
In midday the majnouneh pulses with apian flourishes.

Middle ground, mirror glass is our sea.
Dry as paper lanterns, the fuchsia blossoms flourish.

A missive from what survives us, our vanishing sea.
Names climb the wall and evaporate in whispered flourishes.

From a distance the network of veins, lines in elaborate display, are invisible.
The walls nest beneath bright clusters in cascading flourishes.

And do your leathered hands darken to the color of this earth?
Inkpots and weathered scrolls rely on this leaden air to flourish.

All madness is conjecture; a shepherd stumbling upon sacred verses.
The sea is ringed by a story told with fiery flourishes.

Majnouneh is obstinate charm, is love aflame.
Speak salt, and let them deride the landscapes where memory flourishes.

Slipshape

A golden shovel after Suheir Hammad

A hummingbird lavishes the lilac on
the first morning I am by myself and the
open window ushers in decanted perfume, the sea, rain on the brink
of falling. What slipshape prayers a woman must make of

her body. To write my way out of the stories of war
I wrote the war again and again I wrote its wounds. May
arrives frenzied with questions. Whose children will we
lose at the border? What use is it to remember

what has never ended, to wax elegiac for how
ardently we believed? *This is not who we are* becomes anthem and divine
decree, armor against the living. Here we remain, human
and failing in our florid excesses, our national torpor. Beings

so fragile we might break. Can
we, finally, and can we imagine what our new shapes might be?

III.

We entered September like a defeated battalion.
—Zakaria Mohammed

Letter to June Jordan in September

I cannot pass the anniversary of that first news event of childhood without
returning to your poem. How from my house I watched. And watching,
watched my grief-stricken parents unable to speak. How I leaned into the
screen, the chords of the cries, searching for what was recognizable of fingers
and thighs, of bracelets and moustaches. Macabre arrangement of bodies
with names like our own. I cannot pass without your words. Something
about witnessing twice removed. About distances magnified by the shift into
language. Of dailyness and my own children's vernacular and the machine.
Grinding us all in its jaws. I met a girl from the camp at a reading in Beirut.
She asked if we could talk about the life of poetry. Our families are hauled off
to the world of the dead, and every day it is on screen. In Gaza, we're watching
Ferguson, and in Atlanta we're watching Jerusalem watching Minneapolis
watching. Their weapons and their training programs indistinguishable.
The word *almost* flickers for a nanosecond. Here I note the shelf-life of
self-censorship, legacy of our era. Some days poems are scrawled on pieces of
cardboard and carried on our shoulders at the protest like martyrs. Here I
should say something about hope. Here I should say something about living.

Tantoura Redux

Today the illustrious release their
report, the bodies having been counted,
the sorting and scoring of living wounds
having been judiciously conducted.
Today the telling, removed from our mouths.
As such, will our dead have finally died?
I ask since the most recent arbiters
also assessed, concluded that our dead
had, in fact, died just as we said; we had
seen precisely what has been recounted.
Have our dead now arrived at the threshold
needed to unsettle the sunbathers
stretched out above our families' corpses?
Is the sand hotter beneath their feet? Do we cloud the beachside view?

Apricots

In Rome last summer I learned
that there are seven varieties of apricots,
that they are distinguished not only

by their physical appearance—the freckles on their skin
or the percentage of it that reddens on the vine—
but also by the month in which they ripen.

Damascus, my grandmother's city, is known
for the apricots of its Ghouta valley,
each name ending in a lingering *ee*.

Baladee—the original, descendant
of the ancients of China and the Korean peninsula.
Or Klaabee—the bitter *Armeniaca vulgaris*,

hardy fruit of the eastern steppe.
Or Mawardee—with its flirtatious name
and promise of perfume. That long *ee*

of the possessive claims the apricot
for the country, the animal
wilderness, for water softened with roses.

Last summer in Rome, turning
the corner onto Piazza di Santa Maria,
the clink of the morning's last cappuccino glasses

and low growls of Vespas on the street
gave no indication of the city I would travel to
a few steps forward. I wasn't thinking

of the jam-colored sunsets of Amman, the stone
fruits and wedding music that filled my grandmother's garden,
the serrated leaves of her apricot tree. Then a scent

drifted up from the cobblestones. A thickness,
a palpable haze of flesh beginning
to spoil, of sugar turning in sunlight.

In Amman, a tree like the one leaning
on a wall in the piazza had reigned over
our childhood, baladee apricots like shattered

lanterns aglow at its base, darkening,
gathering droves of ants, the ravenous taking.
Not the perfume of Damascus

mawardee nor the silk handkerchief of blossoms,
not the fruit's citrus kiss. It was the scent of spoiling,
of too much sweetness that claimed me,

long cry at the end of the ballad of old summers.
In Amman, it is known that an apricot harvest
can be ruined by untimely frost and that,

like Rome, the city is built on seven hills.

Gloria

In the late eighties, in the middle of middle
        school we break from studying our ancestors, pass
on the Phoenicians for a while, leave the terraced fields

of Canaan and the hanging gardens of Babylon
        for European History. Miss Magda
is our guide, and she contextualizes

the continent, intertwines it with our own lives, the shapes
        of our maps, the narrowing of our family names. She has
no patience for girls who are charmed by France,

even though a veil of Chanel No. 5
        unfurls over our heads as she enters the room, nor for adults
who praise London's museums. She narrates

a list of our possessions housed there. Miss Magda speaks
        many languages, the queen's English, impeccable
French, maybe others? Her Arabic

is Cairene, her eyeliner distinctly Cleopatran. She speaks مش فارقة معها
        her mind, she names conquerors and the servile
regimes they birthed. She expands the word احتلال

beyond its daily context, locates our current colonizers
        on a continuum of violence, sends us asking
our grandparents for stories. She enacts her name

as she towers over our desks and asks rhetorical questions كثر خير العرب
who translated Aristotle who filled libraries with books
that would later make الرينيسانس بتاعهم *possible.*

In the middle of middle school we are devoted
         to American pop songs a few years after
they top the charts, our childhoods are museums

housing the no-longer hits of the Reagan era. Miss Magda's
         year coincides with our Laura Branigan phase. She can
barely tolerate our tastes. When she cannot escape

playground duty and we are perfecting
         our hair flips, singing Gloria,
she raises a perfect eyebrow in our direction,

and I think maybe even smiles. In class, ever the historian,
         she remarks على فكرة *that's originally an Italian song*
وكانت مش بطالة بس خربوها الأمريكان

Autocorrect

Texting you about floodplains
in the ancient world and *alluvial*
transforms into *I loved*. Your name

cannot stand on its own, predictive
text attaches *-esque*, refashions you
into a quality of yourself, digital

synecdoche. One of my children's names only
appears in ALL CAPS no matter my attempts to save her
in my dictionary; the quietest squalling across the screen.

How do we decide where the ancient begins?

The end of the century in which we came of age
is a rift valley, our memories dropping steeply
at the margins. To describe it to my children I say: there was

no way to reach us if we wandered. No monuments
of our days until the film was developed.
What we knew of time was organized on notecards

in narrow wooden drawers, and we had to take
the bus and walk up several flights of stairs to search it. I text

about what I long for and cannot reach
this year, no nation, just sunlight
on striated hillsides in early spring, and *terra rossa* becomes *terror.*

Do you think the agents assigned to us wear
trench coats and dark sunglasses? Do they write

their reports about us in invisible ink? In ancient times,
the floodplain of the Jordan was covered
in reeds, tamarisk, and willows.

I regret mentioning the tamarisk, how
it ushers in multiple congregations,

concertina wire. How my longings
are only publishable as anti-pastorals,
refined alterations of a text that contend,

collapse. My poem was in that first revelation,
the text confiding that what endures

of the alluvial plain, the earth of ancestry, is love.

Zaghareed

The first time it tumbled out soft-edged imperfect but proof it had lived there all along gleeful and spiraling a girl delighted with her skirt spinning to show her aunts what its glittered tulle could do.

***

The second time was at a wedding the old women louder though they lifted it a young bird trilling on the current bird of more ambition than wingspan.

***

The third time I was alone wondering at my own sounds did they pulse and sway like the women who balance a row of gold coins and a tray of henna on their heads who welcome the bridegroom as he descends the white horse.

***

The fourth time was at a graduation and it gleamed above the thick curls of a name.

***

The fifth time I swallowed it a mouthful of shrapnel as the procession carried the dead boy back to his mother the women's eyes rimmed the color of pomegranates holding her up coaxing it from her clenched jaw.

***

The sixth time was at an airport there were women waiting and when their wait ended and their voices broke the sky I opened my mouth and it held me among them.

***

The seventh time was at a hair salon the seventh time I was already a mother the seventh time the woman who makes the coffee rushed over and said *the bride is leaving now* the seventh time when in my half-knowing I smiled she clarified *her mother is dead. there is no one to send her off. we're going to. can you ululate?* and it was

***

the first time the tears didn't disrupt its flight the whole flock of it loosed from somewhere beneath my rib cage until I was light-headed and the walls hummed with our dancing breath the stand-in mothers in our joy for her until the ivory hem of her veil was no longer visible in the doorway.

Welcome

The air and the memory
of flies are a damp cloak
as the car winds between pomelo groves
and bougainvillea. Is it salt

or is it sand or
is it the armed guards
that thicken the silence inside of you?
An offering of documents

and hours and an excavation of
genealogy may or may not grant you
entry. The roles are preassigned—the smiling soldier
offering water in her chalky Arabic,

the taciturn one with the posture of
an accountant tracing stamps in your passport,
oblivious to the corpulent insect hovering
over his head. Here, everything

is an exercise in endurance. Will you
smile back. Will you lose
your temper. Will you be enticed
by the free Wi-Fi. Asked the same question

for the twentieth time, will you confuse

the names of your great-grandparents, restarting

the clock. Will you fall

down a chute or climb a ladder?

The fly grows louder and more lethargic

as it orbits, grazing the soldier's head,

then zigzagging across the poster

hanging on the wall behind him, like a tiny F-16

casting its ominous shadow

over a sunglossed stretch of Mediterranean,

and the fading letters of welcome

obscuring the shoreline.

Golden

Alweibdeh is definitely the cutest neighborhood we visited.
So much culture!
—American Tourist

Say this girl in earlier editions drowned
in this particular light. Say it's possible

to walk again the roads and uneven pavements
where I and my mother were children.

Say this hillside, its summer
adornments. Say we pass

beneath jasmine, catch its petals
in our hair. Say even the plastic bags caught

in the linden branches. Now the neighbor's
home is a café serving golden milk

to all manner of mercenaries. It was so recently
untranslated, the faces in the windows

knew the stories of the streets below.
Say clotheslines on the one day

water arrives. Say morning newspapers, say lines
of mourners at the funeral tent three days in a row.

Say simmering pots announce their cumin, coriander,
alchemies marbling over a low flame.

Say we don't trend,
say we guard the sites

of memory, smile to ourselves,
pass the falafel place, the tailor, the greengrocer,

neither confirm nor deny.
Say we never exhibit our grandmothers'

sewing machines in a museum,
never donate our parents'

faded love letters.
Say we were unremarkable, huddled

together in modest living rooms, waiting
on a kettle to boil, burning

lemon rind on kerosene stoves.

Crowdsourced

Discard the imperial names of cities and villages.

Share the story of watermelon days, your family's address a Jerusalem

street you won't be allowed to enter.

Say liberation where before you spoke of endings.

Wear a kuffiyeh in the profile picture,

write your name in Arabic in the bio.

Receive private heartfelt messages.

The questions about peace are delivered more artfully.

The questions about freedom rarely arrive.

Occasionally, you are permitted to speak about the dead.

You will be asked if you have family in Gaza.

Not if you have family in Haifa.

Not about Bethlehem. Or Lydd.

You will be lectured about the sanctity

of a university campus where people can exchange ideas

on the ruins of the razed village. You will not be asked

about the village. You are often asked

for your family's hummus recipe.

You are asked about nothing at all.

Share the video. Don't share the video.

Renovate the sites of insomnia.

Continue calling your elected representatives.

Catalog the throngs. Delete the missives.

Find the flag for the rally on Sunday.

Make new signs with the whole map on them.

Sing *janna janna* with a younger chorus.

Fumble the lyrics, but the melody always returns to you.

Dukka

At the restaurant the loudest sound

is the ocean a few blocks away.

A meteor shower is forecast, a once-

in-a-lifetime event, but the freeway flush with headlights

precludes us from viewing. The stars fall

silently over us and the waves and the commuters.

We review the menu. We help the waitress pronounce dukka.

We talk about aging and what is left

to risk. Love

is paying attention, I remark, and you

repeat it to me. Love is also the father

who plants an olive tree for every newborn

trusting they will grow up to harvest it. Love is

the elderly woman who stood inside

Damascus Gate, knowing the settlers

were on a rampage, knowing

what her body would have to endure. Love is a story

we never tire of telling, just as Shireen

told it with a microphone and a camera. Love lives

in many rooms. In the kitchen where Nadia teaches

using only the Arabic names of ingredients. And in the car

where Lema embroiders wine-colored roosters

and cypresses on ancestral linen, waiting

to pick up her children from school.

Love is the children we carried

at the protests, leading their own marches in the rain.

Let the stars fall. I have no idea

what hope is, but our people

have taught me a million ways to love.

Notes & Acknowledgments

The epigraph for the book is from June Jordan's poem "Moving Towards Home," first published in her collection *Living Room*.

The epigraph for section I is from *After the Last Sky* by Edward Said.

"Variations on a Last Chance" and "On the Thirtieth Friday We Consider Plurals" are dedicated to Palestinians who were killed in the Great March of Return, beginning in April 2018.

In "Dialogic" the italicized excerpts are from *The Palestinian Exodus from Galilee in 1948* by Nafez Nazzal and *Sacred Landscape: The Buried History of the Holy Land Since 1948* by Meron Benvenisti.

The epigraph for section II is from "Solo Performance" by Mahmoud Darwish, published in *A'ras*, Beirut: Dar Alwda, 1977.

"In Palestine There" borrows lines and writes with gratitude toward Myung Mi Kim's poems in *Under Flag*.

"Maqluba" is named after a beloved Palestinian dish that is slow-cooked in a pot and then inverted on a serving platter (turned "upside down," the meaning of the name) and garnished with fried almonds.

The epigraph for section III is from an untitled poem by Zakaria Mohammed, from *A Date For The Crows*, my translation.

"Letter to June Jordan in September" writes back with love to Jordan's poem "Moving Towards Home" from her collection *Living Room*.

"A Single Word" is a cento comprised of lines from several of Fady Joudah's translations of Mahmoud Darwish poems, from the collection *The Butterfly's Burden*.

In "Triptych" the materials of the first panel include the Universal Declaration of Human Rights, the Geneva Convention, United Nations Security Resolution 242, and United Nations General Assembly Resolution 194, documents that have long governed Palestinian hope. The second panel is a natural process. The third panel is a cento of Palestinian voices including poets and writers Fadwa Tuqan, Suheir Hammad, Nathalie Handal, Mahmoud Darwish, Naomi Shihab Nye, Samih Al Qassem, Ghassan Zaqtan, and Ghassan Kanafani.

In "Crowdsourced," *janna janna* is an Arabic protest song popular in Palestine and Syria originally composed and sung by Iraqi artist Kareem Al-Iraqi in 1928.

"Dukka" is for Naseem Tuffaha.

Gratitude to Two Sylvias Press, who first published several of these poems, sometimes in different versions, in *Arab in Newsland*, winner of the 2016 Two Sylvias Chapbook Prize, and to the editors of the following journals:

    "Apricots," *New England Review*, June 2018.
    "Autocorrect," *Michigan Quarterly Review*, Summer 2022, winner of
        the Goldstein Poetry Prize.
    "Beit Anya," *West Branch*, September 2021 and *Poetry Daily 2022*.
    "Dendrology," *One Magazine*, Jacar Press, April 2020.
    "Dialogic," *Hayden's Ferry Review*, December 2018.
    "Envelope," *BOAAT*, July 2019.
    "First Generation," *Exposition Review*, June 2023.
    "Fragments from a Sudden Crescendo," *The Rumpus*, May 2021.
    "Gloria," *Poem-A-Day, Poets.org*, September 2018.
    "Iconic," *Mizna*, July 2018 and "Triptych" and "Long Distance,"
        July 2023.
    "In Case of Emergency," *Massachusetts Review*, Summer 2016.
    "In Palestine There," *Green Mountain Review*, September 2021.
    "Letter to June Jordan in September," *The Nation*, January 2022.
    "Madwoman Ghazal," *TriQuarterly Review*, January 2019.
    "Maritime Nocturne," *Gaza Unsilenced*, Just World Books, June 2015.
    "Notes from the Civil Discourse Committee," *Tahoma Literary*
        Review, September 2023.

"On the Thirtieth Friday We Consider Plurals" and "To Be Self-Evident," *West Branch,* Winter 2024.

"Other Words for Blue," *Raleigh Review,* January 2020.

"Slipshape," *Solstice Literary Magazine,* February 2021.

"Portraits of Lights," as "Three Photographs," *Tinderbox Poetry Journal,* July 2018.

"Variations on a Last Chance," semi-finalist for the *Crab Creek Review Prize,* Fall 2018.

"This Day Our Daily Bread," and "Threads," *Waxwing Literary Journal,* 2018.

"When the Sky Is No Longer" was first published in *Arab in Newsland,* Two Sylvias Press, 2017.

"Zaghareed," *Redivider,* June 2018.

Lena Khalaf Tuffaha is a poet, essayist, and translator. She is the author of *Water & Salt* (Red Hen), which won the 2018 Washington State Book Award, and *Kaan & Her Sisters* (Trio House Press). She is also the author of two chapbooks, *Arab in Newsland*, winner of the 2016 Two Sylvias Prize, and *Letters from the Interior* (Diode Editions). Tuffaha served as the inaugural Poet-In-Residence at Open Books: A Poem Emporium, in Seattle in 2017-18. She is the recipient of a 2019 Artist Trust fellowship, and her writing has been published in journals including *Los Angeles Review of Books*, *Michigan Quarterly Review*, *The Nation*, and *Poets.org* and in anthologies including *The Long Devotion*, *Alone Together*, and *Bettering American Poetry*. She is the curator and translator of the *Poems from Palestine* series at *The Baffler* magazine. For more about her work, visit www.lenakhalaftuffaha.com.